I Can Wash My Hands

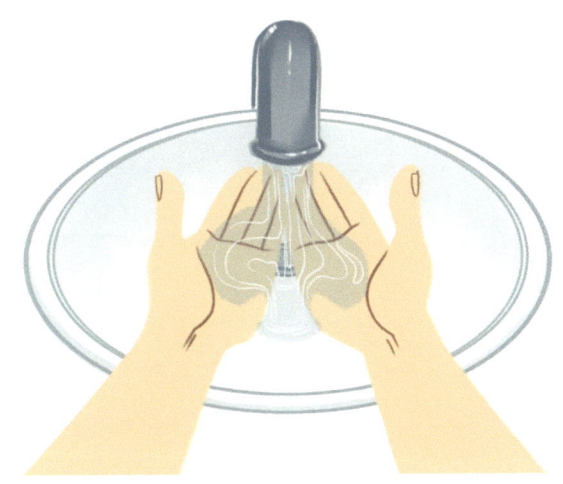

Written by Chemise Taylor

Illustrated by Alexis B. Taylor

Core 6 Book
Workbook Activities
Visual Task Analysis
Flashcards
App

Copyright © 2019 by My Skills Books

Published by My Skills Books

All rights reserved. No part of this publication may be reproduced, distributed, or transmitted in any form or by any means, including photocopying, recording, or other electronic or mechanical methods, without the prior written permission of the publisher, except in the case of brief quotations embodied in critical reviews and certain other noncommercial uses permitted by copyright law.

First Printing, 2019.

ISBN: 978-1-951573-03-4

www.myskillsbooks.com

There are many reasons to wash my hands.

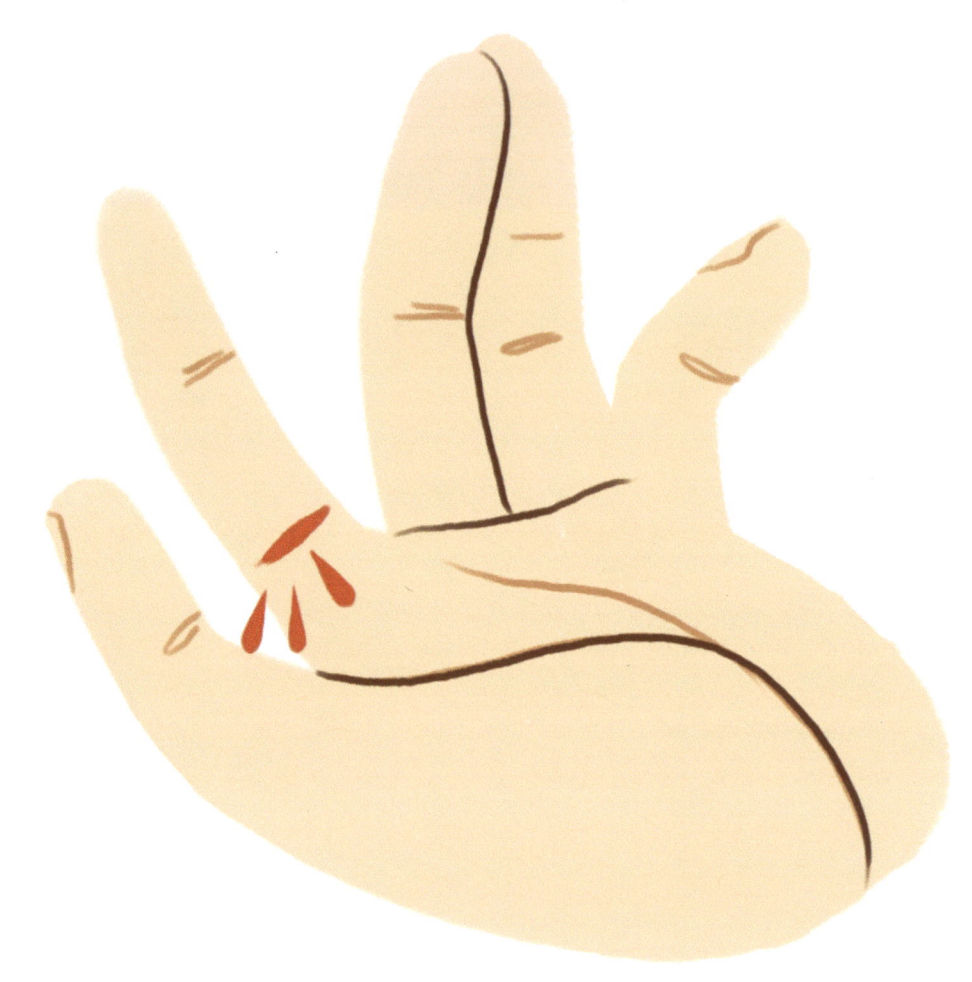

If I cut my hand or I am bleeding.

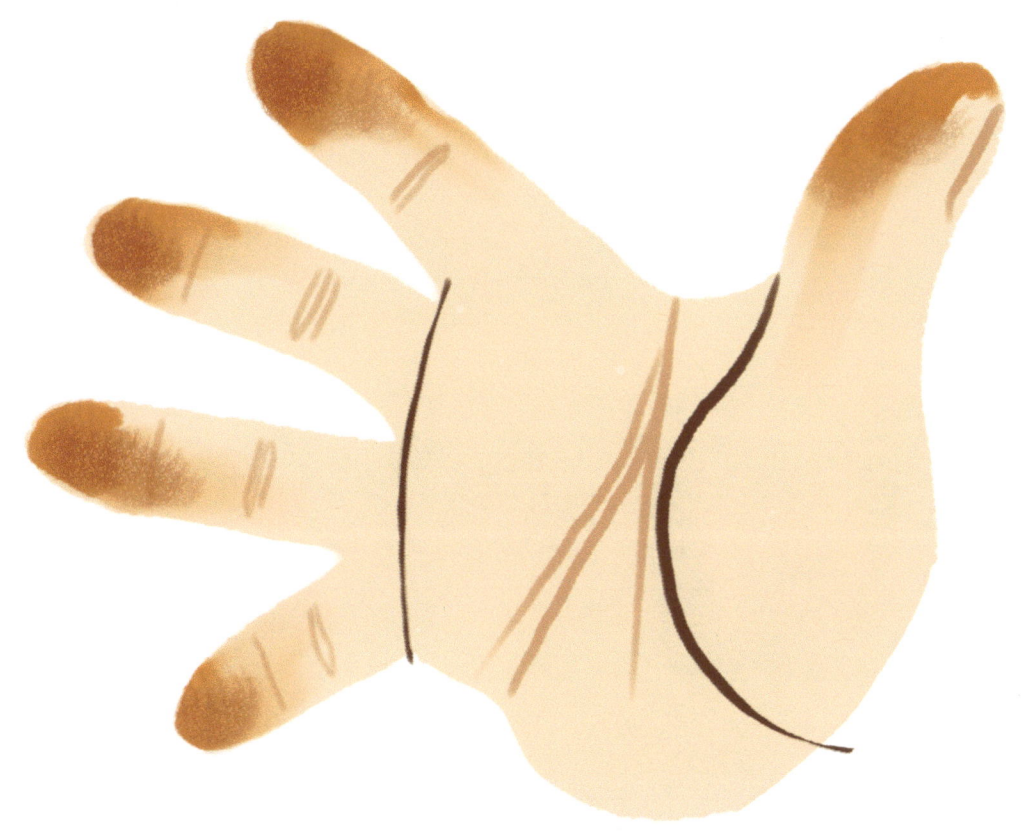

If I touch something dirty.

If my hands get messy while playing.

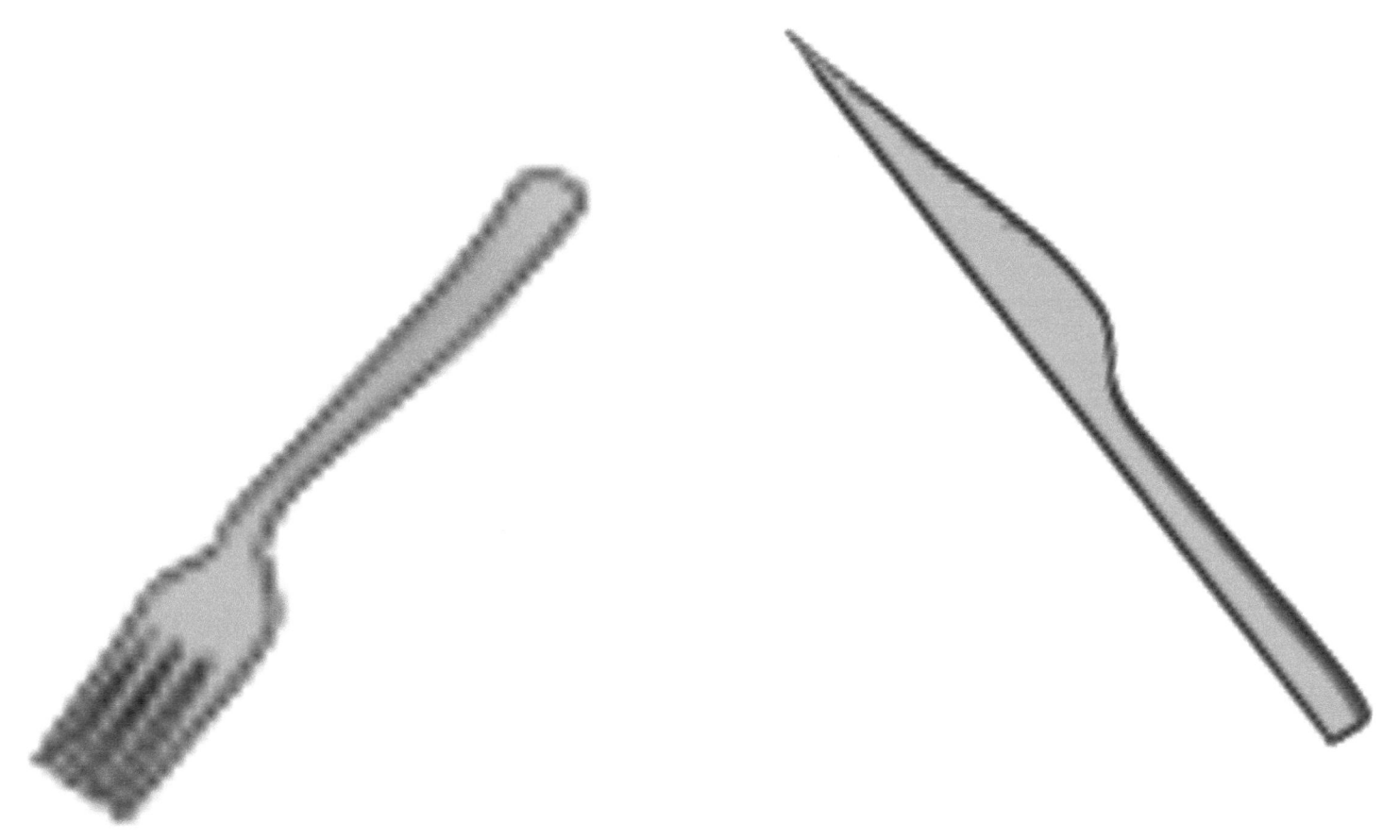

Before I eat.

After I use the bathroom.

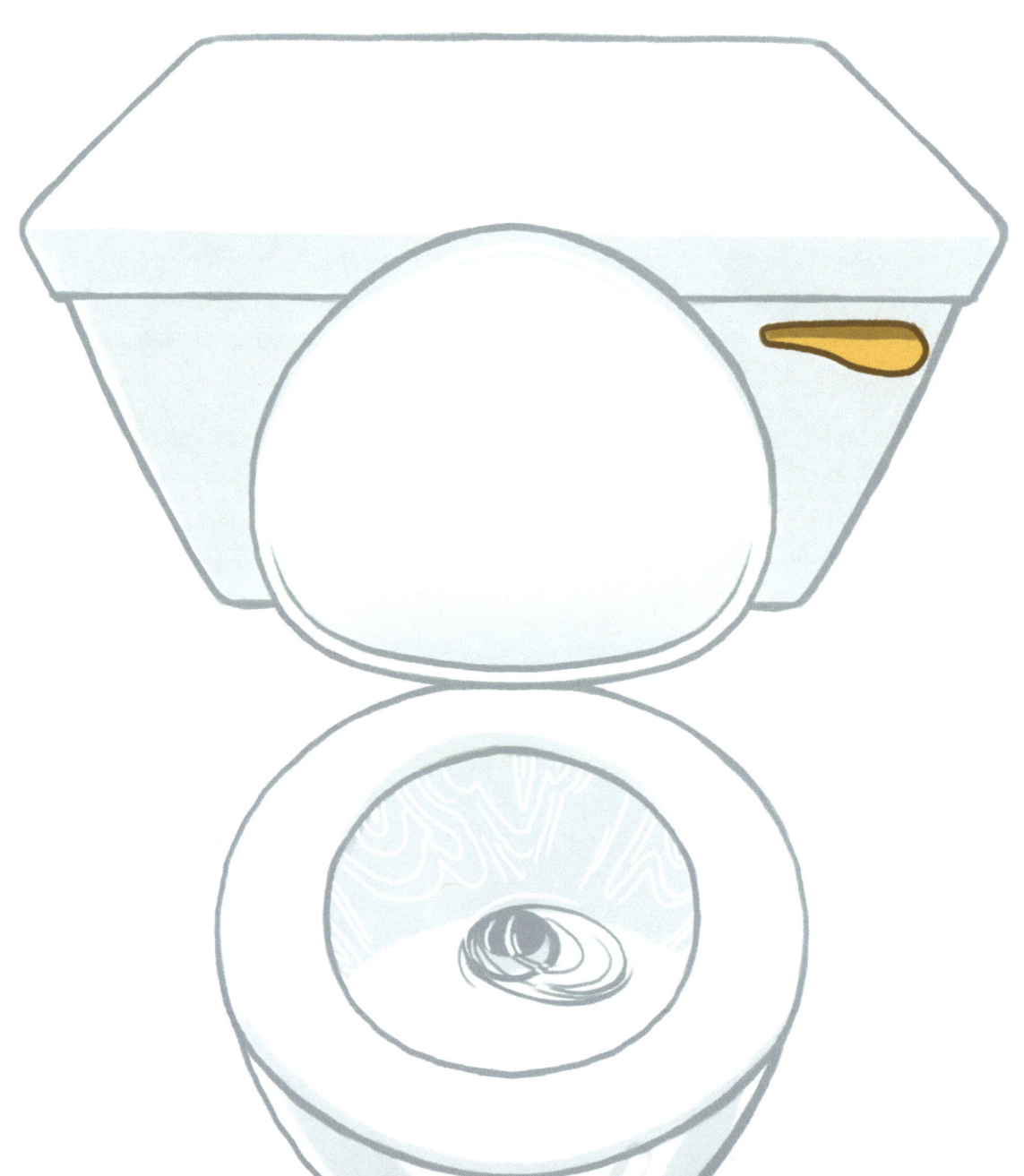

My hands are stinky and dirty.
I need to wash my hands.

I go to the sink and turn on the faucet.

I wet my hands under running water.

I rub the soap onto my hands to clean the dirt away.

I wash my hands for....

20 to 30 seconds

I rinse the soap off my hands with water.

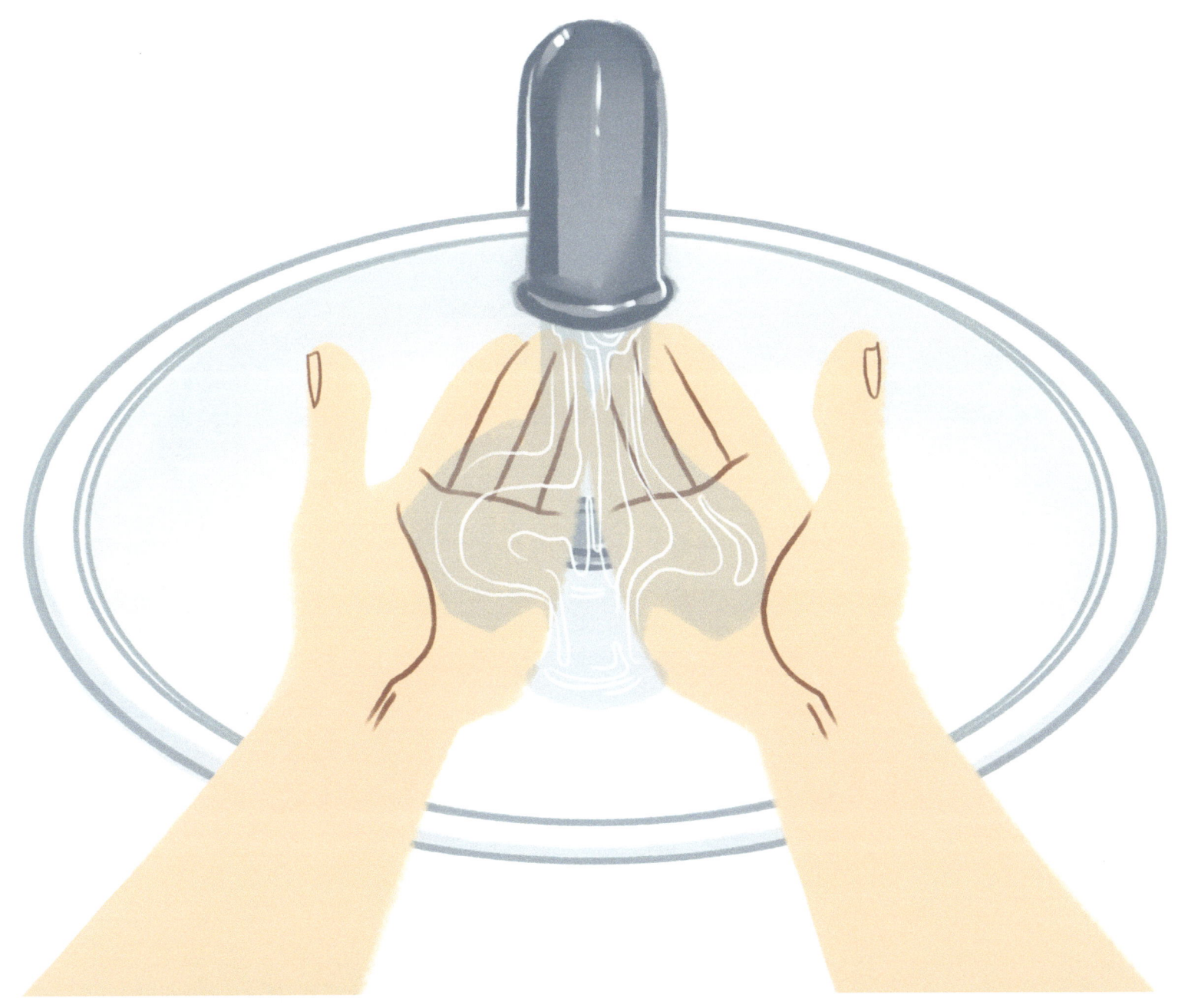

I dry my hands with a towel.

Look! Now my hands are all clean!

Book Details

Story Word Count: 121

Key Words: Wash, Hands, Soap. Water, Sink, Lather, Towel, Dry

Comprehension Check

- What was the story about?
- What should you do if your get a cut or get dirt on your hands?
- What does she rub onto her hands?

Reading Award

This certificate goes to:

_____

for reading "I Can Wash My Hands"

Good Job!

More books, apps and resources at myskillsbooks.com

www.ingramcontent.com/pod-product-compliance
Lightning Source LLC
Chambersburg PA
CBHW042108090526
44591CB00004B/49